The BOY WHO INVENTED the POPSICLE

The Cool Science Behind Frank Epperson's Famous Frozen Treat

Anne Renaud

Milan Pavlović

Kids Can Press

Frank William Epperson knew what he wanted to be when he grew up.

And everyone in Frank's family knew, too. Because in case they forgot, he reminded them — often.

When not busy with his schoolwork
or chores, Frank could be found ...

adventuring with his brother Cray,

practicing his cornet,

or learning magic tricks.

He also pondered important questions.

Do ants have ears?

Do goldfish sleep?

Do woodpeckers get headaches from pecking all day?

But Frank's favorite pastime was
inventing. And to invent, Frank knew
he had to experiment. So off he would
go to his laboratory — his back porch.
There, he doodled and designed.

Tinkered and tested.

Analyzed and scrutinized.

By the time Frank was ten years old, he had already masterminded his first invention: a handcar with two handles. At twice the speed of a regular one-handled handcar, Frank whizzed down the streets of his neighborhood.

Hot dog!

Frank also experimented with liquids.

Why Won't They Play Together?
How to do your own experiment with liquids

Stuff you need:

- 125 mL (½ c.) cooking oil
- 125 mL (½ c.) water
- a drinking glass

What to do:

1. Pour the cooking oil into a glass.
2. Add the water.
3. Mix the two liquids together.
4. Wait 2 minutes.

What happened?

The oil rose above the water because it is less dense (lighter for its size) than water. No matter how much you mix these two liquids, they will always separate. Why? Just like magnets are attracted to other magnets, water molecules are attracted to other water molecules. But oil molecules and water molecules are not attracted to each other.

One more thing:

Food coloring is made of water. See what happens when you add a few drops of food coloring to the glass. The drops will slowly travel through the oil and only mix with the water.

Molecules are like building blocks. Just as a house is made of bricks, you and I and almost everything on Earth are made up of minuscule particles called molecules. Molecules are so small they can only be seen with a very powerful microscope.

But what Frank loved most was experimenting with flavored soda waters. The kind that hissed and wheezed when he held a glassful to his ear, and sent tangy bubbles galloping across his tongue with every gulp.

Frank had his heart set on inventing the yummiest, most thirst-quenching, lip-smacking soda water drink ever!

So off Frank would go to the corner store to buy the flavored soda water powders he needed for his experiments. Often with his little brother Cray tagging along.

Cray was a handy taster for Frank's concoctions.
Some of his attempts were unsuccessful ... you could
even say they were disastrous!
But Frank just kept on trying.

A Whole Lot of Fizzing Going On
How to make your own lemon-flavored soda water

Stuff you need:

- 60 mL (4 tbsp.) lemon juice
- 250 mL (1 c.) water
- a drinking glass
- 2.5 mL (½ tsp.) baking soda
- 5 mL (1 tsp.) sugar

What to do:

1. Pour the lemon juice into the glass.
2. Add the water.
3. Add the baking soda and mix well. You should see some fizzing action going on.
4. Now taste your lemonade. You can add the sugar to sweeten.

What happened?

The baking soda reacted with the lemon juice and created a gas called carbon dioxide. This is what makes the fizz.

One more thing:

Try this experiment with other citrus fruits like limes, oranges and grapefruit.

One day, Frank and the other children in his neighborhood decided to build a miniature amusement park. There was a theater, a merry-go-round and a scenic railway.

Frank was assigned the soda water stand — which suited him just fine. He could share his soda water creations with all his friends.

FRANK'S SODA WATER

It was also around this time that something peculiar happened: the temperature dipped ... then plunged.

This would not have been unusual had Frank lived in Moose Jaw, Saskatchewan, or Pocatello, Idaho, where it could be bitterly cold in winter. But he lived in San Francisco, California, where only rarely did the temperature drop below freezing.

So Frank tried another experiment. He left a glass of flavored soda water outside overnight.

When he woke the next morning, Frank ran to his back porch to discover his soda water had frozen solid. He could no longer sip it. He had to lick it — like a lollipop!

Frank had invented a frozen drink on a stick!

As he grew older, Frank's invention did not melt from his memory. He just tucked it away in a corner of his mind. And there it stayed while he and his sweetheart, Mary Frances, began raising their gaggle of children.

But when Frank noticed more and more people
eating chocolate-covered ice-cream bars, off he went
to his laboratory — now his garage — to experiment.

Frank found a way to make many of
his drinks on a stick at the same time.

With test tubes to mold them,

wooden sticks to hold them,

and a cool way to freeze them.

For Frank's drinks on a stick to freeze, they had to be cold — very cold. Colder than 0°C (32°F), the freezing point of water. Why? Because their ingredients, like sugar and flavoring, lowered their freezing point.

So what did Frank do? He built a freezing box that held dozens of test tubes suspended in a mixture of crushed ice and salt. Frank knew that salt lowered the freezing point of water, and that salty water froze at a much lower temperature than plain tap water. The salt-and-ice mixture would be colder than 0°C (32°F).

The Big Freeze

How to show that salt lowers the freezing point of water

Stuff you need:

- 2 drinking glasses
- 60 mL (4 tbsp.) salt
- 500 mL (2 c.) lukewarm water

What to do:

1. Pour 250 mL (1 c.) of lukewarm water into each glass.
2. Add the salt to one of the glasses and mix well until the salt is fully dissolved.
3. Put both glasses of water into the freezer and wait 3 hours.

What happened?

The plain tap water froze, but the salty water did not. Why? Water becomes ice when it reaches 0°C (32°F). But if there is sodium chloride, also known as salt, in the water, it lowers the water's freezing point. The temperature of the salty water needs to be colder than 0°C (32°F) for it to freeze.

One more thing:

Touch the glass of salty water. It feels colder than the glass of frozen water. Cool!

Frank's drinks on a stick also had to freeze quickly. If they froze too slowly, the sugar and flavoring, which were heavier than water, settled at the bottom of the test tubes, leaving just flavorless frozen water at the top. Frank wanted his treats to have the same tasty flavor throughout.

The salt-and-crushed-ice mixture surrounding the test tubes was so cold it froze the liquid inside the tubes in minutes.

A Frozen Treat in a Flash!

How to make your own frozen treat in only five minutes

Stuff you need:

- 125 mL (½ c.) of your favorite fruit juice
- 10 large ice cubes
- 250 mL (1 c.) salt
- 250 mL (1 c.) water
- a small plastic resealable bag
- a large plastic resealable bag
- oven mitts

What to do:

1. Pour the juice into the small plastic bag. Try to remove the air from the bag and make sure it is well sealed.
2. Pour the ice cubes, water and salt into the large plastic bag.
3. Put the smaller bag of juice inside the larger bag. Make sure the larger bag is well sealed.
4. Put on your oven mitts and shake the bag back and forth for about 5 minutes to mix the ice, water and salt around the smaller bag.

What happened?

As you saw in the previous experiment, salt lowers the freezing point of water. This means salty water gets much colder than 0°C (32°F). When you shake the large bag back and forth, and work the ice, water and salt mixture around the smaller bag of juice, this mixture gets colder and colder and the juice freezes. This is why oven mitts come in handy!

One more thing:

Best to shake the bag over the sink to avoid a mess.

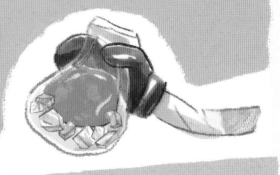

Frank named his invention the Ep-sicle and began selling it for a nickel at county fairs and beaches. In the evenings, his children helped him roll the nickels he had earned.

Frank had a clever way to encourage shop owners to sell his frozen treats. For several weeks in a row, he sent one of his children into a store to buy an Ep-sicle. Each week, the shop owner had to tell a different child that Ep-sicles were not sold in the store. Frank would then visit the store himself and ask the shop owner to stock his treats. Of course the owner agreed — after having had so many requests!

Frank's children were always keen to sample their father's confections.

And with all of them clamoring for their pop's tasty fabrications, in time, the name of Frank's invention changed to ...

Author's Note

Francis (Frank) William Epperson was born on August 11, 1894, in Willows, California.

He was an inventor at heart and loved to experiment. By the age of ten, Frank had made himself a handcar operated with two handles. The following year, he left his glass of soda water on the back porch and woke up to a frozen treat that eventually became known around the world as the Popsicle®. And in case you are wondering why Frank did not put his glass in the freezer … well, that is because modern home refrigerators with freezer compartments did not become popular in North America until the 1940s.

Frank left school at fourteen to work in his father's chinaware factory. Four years later, he eloped with his sweetheart, sixteen-year-old Mary Frances Williams. Together they opened a business painting china dishes, which Frank sold door-to-door. Then, during the First World War, he worked as a machinist foreman in the shipyards.

By the time Frank was twenty-five, he and Mary Frances had five children — including two sets of twins! Although Frank had secured employment as a real estate developer by then, he always welcomed the opportunity to make extra money for his growing family, which would eventually number nine children.

In the early 1920s, Frank noticed that a chocolate-covered ice-cream bar had started gaining popularity — and that is when he remembered his childhood invention. Using six-inch glass test tubes as a mold, and sticks of wood from the Diamond Match Company, Frank began making his frozen treat — which he named the Ep-sicle — in large quantities.

He first tested out the Ep-sicle in 1922 at a Firemen's Ball at the Neptune Beach ballroom in Alameda, California. He and his wife walked around eating one frozen treat after another in the hopes of drawing the attention of those in attendance. It worked.

By 1923, the treat was renamed Popsicle® because Frank's children repeatedly asked for their pop's "'sicles."

To ensure repeat customers, Frank printed "One free popsicle" on every tenth Popsicle® stick.

In 1924, Frank finally applied for patents for his "frozen confectionery" and his "confectionery-making apparatus." Eventually, he sold his rights to the Popsicle® for $50 000 to pay off some debts and help his family through financial hardship. Although he later regretted this, given the wealth the rights could have brought him and his family over time, he was always quick to remind his children that what was important was not what they had, but who they were.

In his lifetime, Frank invented a number of other things, including a dictionary to simplify spelling, called *Spel*, a powdered drink named Hi-Dry, a sunscreen called Vitano, a signaling device for ships to warn them of approaching danger, as well as a rotary engine for airplanes. He also designed and built two of his homes, both of which were inspired by castles.

Frank Epperson died on October 22, 1983. He was eighty-nine years old.

Today, with more than thirty flavors available, hundreds of millions of Popsicle® ice pops are slurped every year throughout the world. Frank Epperson's frozen treat, invented in 1905 when he was only eleven, is now well over a century old.

Frank (right) and his younger brother Cray (left) practicing their cornets, circa 1907. Photo courtesy of Jack Epperson.

Frank selling his Popsicles®. Salinas, California, July 20, 1923. This is said to be the very first photograph of Popsicles® being sold. Photo courtesy of Chris Lang.

Frank and his wife, Mary Frances, with eight of their nine children, circa 1937. Front row: Frank holding Marge, Teresa (standing), Joe and Mary. Back row: John, Frank Jr., Sister Serena (Donna), Don and George. Photo courtesy of Jack Epperson.

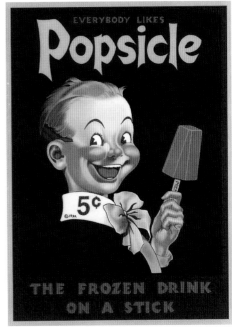

Vintage Popsicle® advertisement. Reproduced with the kind permission of Unilever PLC and Group companies.

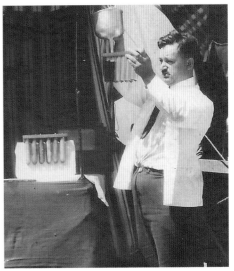

Frank making his Popsicles® at his stand. Salinas, California, July 20, 1923. Photo courtesy of Chris Lang.

To Frank Epperson, who knew that to invent he had to experiment — A.R.

For Leo, my blue-eyed angel — M.P.

Published in Canada and the U.S. by Kids Can Press Ltd.
25 Dockside Drive, Toronto, ON M5A 0B5

Kids Can Press is a Corus Entertainment Inc. company

www.kidscanpress.com

The artwork in this book was rendered in mixed media — pencil, color inks and digitally.
The text is set in Boudoir.

Edited by Jennifer Stokes
Designed by Marie Bartholomew
Title type hand-lettered by Milan Pavlović

Printed and bound in Paju, Republic of Korea, in 10/2022 by Imago

CM 19 0 9 8 7 6 5 4

Library and Archives Canada Cataloguing in Publication

Title: The boy who invented the Popsicle : the cool science behind Frank Epperson's famous frozen treat / Anne Renaud ; [illustrated by] Milan Pavlović.
Names: Renaud, Anne, 1957– author. | Pavlović, Milan (Illustrator), illustrator.
Description: Includes bibliographical references.
Identifiers: Canadiana 20189060867 | ISBN 9781525300288 (hardcover)
Subjects: LCSH: Epperson, Frank, 1894–1983 — Juvenile literature. | LCSH: Children as inventors — California — Biography — Juvenile literature. | LCSH: Ice pops — History — Juvenile literature. | LCSH: Food — Experiments — Juvenile literature.Classification: LCC TX796.I46 R46 2019 | DDC j641.86/3092 — dc23

Kids Can Press gratefully acknowledges that the land on which our office is located is the traditional territory of many nations, including the Mississaugas of the Credit, the Anishnabeg, the Chippewa, the Haudenosaunee and the Wendat peoples, and is now home to many diverse First Nations, Inuit and Métis peoples.

We thank the Government of Ontario, through Ontario Creates; the Ontario Arts Council; the Canada Council for the Arts; and the Government of Canada for supporting our publishing activity.

Acknowledgments

I am deeply indebted to the following family members of Frank W. Epperson, who graciously shared their history with me. To Frank's three surviving children, Joe, Marge and Teresa, for imparting precious memories of their father. To granddaughters Chris Lang and Barbe Epperson Seal, and grandsons Jack Epperson and Ian Epperson, for sharing their grandfather's written memoirs, business papers and photographs. And to Nigel Penney, for reviewing the scientific passages of my manuscript. This book would not have had a birthday without your help. I am also grateful to Unilever PLC and its group companies for permission to use the trademarked name Popsicle® in this book. Finally, to my editor Jennifer Stokes, for always being cool and never frosty.

Bibliography

Emmins, Colin. *Soft Drinks*, Shire Publications Ltd., 1991

Frank William Epperson memoirs, miscellaneous personal papers and letters, 1922-1959

Frank W. Epperson Obituary, *New York Times*, October 27, 1983

"Meet the Popsicle's Father," *San Francisco Chronicle*, August 31, 1971

"My Pop Invented the Popsicle ... By Accident," *Reminisce Magazine*, July/August 1992

"Sicle saga stirs son of Popsicle inventor," *San Rafael News Pointer*, October 19, 1994

"Son honors Pop for ice treat," *Marin Independent Journal*, October 11, 1994

Tucker, Tom. *The Stories of Twenty American Inventors*, Farras, Straus & Giroux, 1995

United States Patent 1,505,592 – Issued August 19, 1924

United States Patent 1,734,765 – Issued November 5, 1929

U.S. Department of Agriculture, Weather Bureau, Voluntary Observers' Meteorological Record, January 1905